PRESIDENTS OF THE U.S.A.

John Quincy Adams

OUR SIXTH PRESIDENT

by Gerry and Janet Souter

THE CHILD'S WORLD®

The Child's World

PUBLISHED IN THE UNITED STATES OF AMERICA

THE CHILD'S WORLD®
1980 Lookout Drive • Mankato, MN 56003-1705
800-599-READ • www.childsworld.com

ACKNOWLEDGMENTS
The Child's World®: Mary Berendes, Publishing Director

Creative Spark: Mary McGavic, Project Director; Melissa McDaniel, Editorial
Director; Deborah Goodsite, Photo Research

The Design Lab: Kathleen Petelinsek, Design; Gregory Lindholm, Page Production

Content Adviser: David R. Smith, Adjunct Assistant Professor of History,
University of Michigan–Ann Arbor

PHOTOS
Cover and page 3: White House Historical Association (White House Collection),
(detail); White House Historical Association (White House Collection)

Interior: Alamy: 15 (North Wind Picture Archives); The Art Archive: 4 (Culver
Pictures), 36 and 39; Art Resource, NY: 10 (National Portrait Gallery, Smithsonian
Institution) 16, 18 and 38 (Smithsonian American Art Museum, Washington,
DC); Corbis: 5, 20, 34 (Bettmann), 24 (Corbis); The Granger Collection, New
York: 6, 8, 19, 21, 22, 25, 26, 33 and 39, 35, 37; iStockphoto: 44 (Tim Fan);
National Park Service: 17, 23, 28, 29 top, 29 center, 29 bottom, 31 (Adams
National Historical Park); Naval Historical Center: 11 (Photo #KN-4781);
Picture History: 9 and 38, 13, 30; Photo Researchers, Inc.: 32; SuperStock: 14
(SuperStock, Inc.); U.S. Air Force photo: 45; White House Historical Association
(White House Collection): 12 (detail).

LIBRARY OF CONGRESS CATALOGING-IN-PUBLICATION DATA
Souter, Gerry.
  John Quincy Adams / by Gerry and Janet Souter.
    p. cm. — (Presidents of the U.S.A.)
  Includes bibliographical references and index.
  ISBN 978–1–60253–035–5 (library bound : alk. paper)
1. Adams, John Quincy, 1767–1848—Juvenile literature. 2. Presidents—United
States—Biography—Juvenile literature. I. Souter, Janet, 1940– II. Title. III. Series.

E377.S7 2008
973.5'5092—dc22
  [B]
                                        2008004369

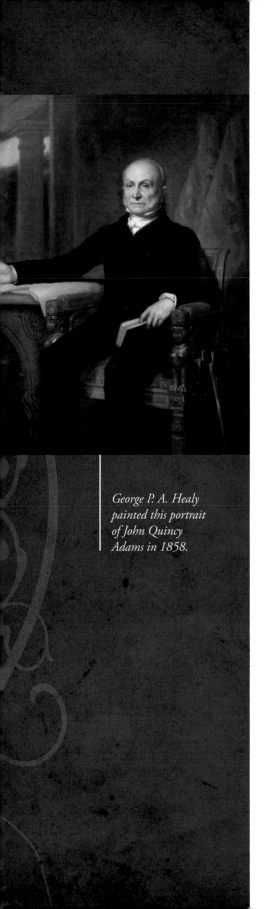

George P. A. Healy
painted this portrait
of John Quincy
Adams in 1858.

TABLE OF CONTENTS

IN HIS FATHER'S FOOTSTEPS

The path in life that John Quincy Adams would follow took shape the moment his parents knew they had a son. He was born on July 11, 1767, on the family farm. The Adamses lived in the town of Braintree, Massachusetts. This area would later become part of Quincy, Massachusetts. John Adams, John Quincy Adams's father, would soon help the American colonies become independent from Great Britain. He would go on to become the second president of the United States.

But when John Quincy was born, John Adams was a little-known country lawyer. The United States had not yet declared its independence. Still, the family dreamed of achieving great things. Devoting one's life to **politics** became a family tradition.

Abigail Adams, John Quincy Adams's mother, came from a leading family in Massachusetts.

John Adams was elected to the **Continental Congress** in 1774. He soon left for Philadelphia, Pennsylvania, where the Congress met. He gave his wife, Abigail, careful instructions about how to raise their children. In one letter, Adams wrote that it was her duty to shape "the minds and manners of our children." John Adams wanted his children not only to be good but also to succeed. He believed that for them to succeed, Abigail had to teach them to work hard and keep busy.

Six-year-old John Quincy thought about this advice. He wrote a letter to his father, saying he had spent too much time playing and having fun. "There

John Adams (far left) was on the committee that wrote the Declaration of Independence. Here, the members of the committee submit the Declaration to the Continental Congress.

is a great deal of room for me to grow better," he said. Throughout his life, John Quincy would always feel he could do better. He would always worry that he was not working hard enough.

On April 19, 1775, the American **Revolution** began. That June, John Quincy held his mother's hand and climbed nearby Penn Hill. They could see the smoke of gunpowder drift across Bunker Hill, where British and American soldiers were in battle. They listened to the booms of cannons being fired. Watching the Revolution unfold so close to home frightened John Quincy, but it also excited him. He began to understand how strongly Americans wanted independence.

The Battle of Bunker Hill was the first major battle of the American Revolution. In the battle, the American troops showed they were the equal of British troops.

The Revolution was expensive and difficult. Americans needed more soldiers and supplies. In 1778, John Quincy's father traveled across the Atlantic Ocean to ask the French king for help. John Adams brought his bright 10-year-old son with him to act as his secretary. It was John Quincy's first job in politics.

John Quincy enrolled at school in France and began studying the French language. In a letter to Abigail, John Adams bragged that their son "learned more French in one day than I could learn in a week."

John and John Quincy soon returned to America. They were happy to see their family again. But not long after they arrived, the Continental Congress had a new job for John Adams. In 1780, he was on his way back to France. This time, both John Quincy and his younger brother, Charles, went with their father. John Quincy again worked as his father's secretary.

At age 14, he traveled to St. Petersburg, Russia, to work for a U.S. **diplomat.** At that time, foreign diplomats usually spoke to each other in French. The man asked John Quincy to come with him to Russia because the young boy spoke French perfectly. He would be the diplomat's **translator.**

The following year, John Quincy toured much of Europe by himself. He ended up in the Hague, a city in the Netherlands where his father was working. He again served as his father's secretary. Finally, in 1785, they returned to the United States. By that time, John Quincy, still a teenager, had already been working and traveling in Europe for many years.

John Quincy had his first job by age 10. He was the family "post rider." He galloped nine miles (14 km) on horseback to pick up the family's mail.

As a young boy, John Quincy read the plays and poetry of William Shakespeare. He also studied Greek and Latin.

John Quincy soon entered Harvard College in Cambridge, Massachusetts. It was the finest college in the country. He studied there for two years before graduating in 1787.

He hoped to become a lawyer like his father. He moved to Connecticut to work for a lawyer while he studied law. One year later, John Quincy Adams opened his first law office.

By this time, the United States had gained its independence. In 1789, George Washington became the nation's first president. At the same time, John Adams became the first vice president. While working as a lawyer, John Quincy Adams found time to write newspaper articles about the government. President Washington read many of these. He recognized young

John Quincy attended Harvard College, just as his father had years before. John Quincy's travels through Europe had made him different from the other students. One remarked that John Quincy was "stiff and formal."

Adams's talent with words. He knew that John Quincy had spent much of his life in foreign countries and spoke many languages. President Washington believed Adams could help the country. He appointed John Quincy **minister** to the Netherlands.

At the age of 26, John Quincy Adams was well on his way to a successful career. His family was proud and hopeful, certain that he would become an important leader, just like his father. "All my hopes are in him," wrote John Adams of his son, "both for my family and country."

In 1792, Braintree was renamed Quincy in honor of Colonel John Quincy. Colonel Quincy was a great-grandfather of John Quincy Adams. The city's name is pronounced "KWIN-zee" rather than "KWIN-see," because that is how Colonel Quincy pronounced his last name.

ADVENTURES AT SEA

In 1778, John Adams was sent to France on a special mission. His task was to convince the French king to help the American colonies win the Revolution. Adams decided to take 10-year-old John Quincy (below) with him.

On the night of February 13, Adams bundled his young son in a blanket, and they boarded a ship called the *Boston* (right). This ship would take them across the Atlantic, but they had no idea how difficult the crossing would be.

First, a group of British ships chased the *Boston* for two days after it left the harbor. Then, the wintry crossing of the Atlantic Ocean was terrifying. Icy winds and high waves tossed the ship to and fro. At one point, a lightning bolt struck the ship, injuring more than 20 sailors. Eventually, the *Boston* sailed free of the storm, only to discover a British ship sailing nearby. The

captain of the *Boston* wanted to attack the British craft, but
the decision belonged to John Adams. As young John Quincy
watched the sails of the distant ship, his father ordered
the attack.

John Quincy was sent below deck, but he watched the
battle through an open porthole. Cannonballs whizzed across
the ship's deck, just missing John Adams's head. Finally, the
British ship gave up.

Still later in the voyage, an officer was hurt while firing
a signal gun. Young John Quincy watched his father hold the
officer's head while the ship's surgeon cut off the man's badly
injured arm. By the time the *Boston* reached France, John
Quincy Adams had received an education in war and survival.

CHAPTER TWO

A CAREER IN POLITICS

During his stay in the Netherlands, John Quincy Adams traveled to England. There he met Louisa Catherine Johnson, the daughter of a U.S. diplomat. She was charming and independent. She was also from a wealthy family. John Quincy knew that her wealth could help him in his career. Abigail Adams disapproved of Louisa. Abigail believed that, although Louisa could dance and sing, she knew nothing about how to live on a diplomat's limited income. Abigail was convinced that Louisa and her fancy way of life would ruin her son. Defying his mother's wishes, John Quincy asked Louisa to marry him, and she accepted. Not long after, her father announced that he had lost all his money. John Quincy was disappointed, for the family money would have helped his career in politics. Nevertheless, he and Louisa married in 1797.

*John Quincy Adams
was quiet and serious.*

This portrait of Louisa Adams was painted in 1816. Louisa was at the center of the Washington social scene during her husband's early years in Washington.

By then, John Adams was president. He appointed his son the U.S. minister to Prussia, which was part of the kingdom of Germany. John Quincy and Louisa packed their bags and traveled to Berlin, the capital of Prussia. They stayed there until the spring of 1801. Then they set sail for the United States with their infant son, George Washington Adams. They would eventually have two more sons, John and Charles. Louisa, their only daughter, died as an infant.

Back in Massachusetts, John Quincy served briefly as a state senator. Then, in 1802, he was elected to the U.S. Senate. At the time, the two major **political parties** in the United States were the Federalists and

Although Louisa Adams's father was an American, she was born and raised in London, England. She is the only foreign-born first lady in U.S. history.

the Democratic-Republicans. The Federalists controlled the Senate, and John Quincy's father was a Federalist. President Thomas Jefferson led the Democratic-Republicans. The two parties often had bitter disagreements.

The Federalists had helped John Quincy Adams get elected to the Senate. They hoped that he would support them. After all, his father was a Federalist. But John Quincy was an independent thinker. He followed his own beliefs and often opposed the Federalists. For example, he supported Jefferson's decision to purchase a huge piece of land from the French. The deal, called the Louisiana Purchase, more than doubled the size

John Adams, a Federalist, became the second president of the United States by defeating Thomas Jefferson, a Democratic-Republican. But Jefferson served as Adams's vice president. According to the rules of the day, the presidential **candidate** who came in second became vice president. This process put people who opposed each other politically in charge of the country. Today, the president and vice president are always from the same party.

John Quincy Adams sometimes sided with Thomas Jefferson (right), angering his father and other Federalists.

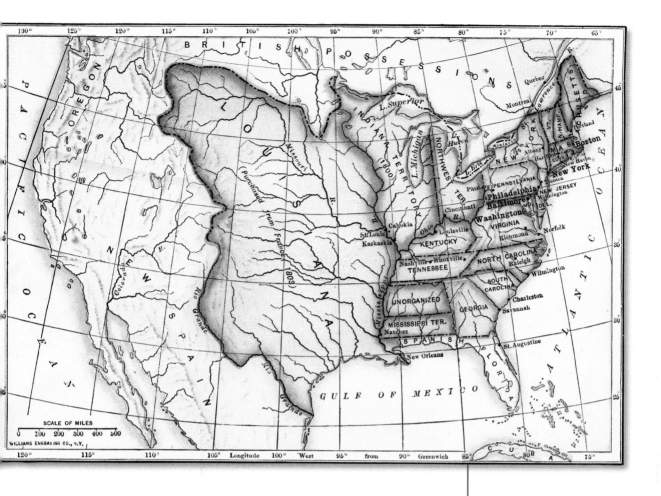

of the United States. The Federalists were furious that Adams would support anything proposed by Jefferson, the enemy of their party. John Quincy learned he could make enemies by thinking for himself.

John Quincy also sided with Jefferson on the **Embargo** Act of 1807. The British had been attacking U.S. ships at sea. To stop this, Jefferson urged passage of the Embargo Act. The act barred American ships from taking goods to Great Britain—or to anywhere else in Europe. It also barred European ships from entering American ports. Jefferson believed the embargo might force Britain to leave American ships

When the United States made the Louisiana Purchase, it added land from the Mississippi River to the Rocky Mountains.

15

An American ship (right) captures a British ship during the War of 1812. The war lasted until 1814.

alone. He thought the British would lose money without American goods. Eventually, they would want American goods badly enough that they would stop attacking American ships.

The Federalists were against the embargo. They were angry that John Quincy was supporting Jefferson yet again. But he would not let the Federalists tell him what to do or how to think. When Federalists met in Boston in 1808, they decided to support a different candidate for the Senate in the next election. Adams felt it was impossible to continue his work after such an insult, so he **resigned** from the Senate.

Adams spent a relaxing year reading and gardening in Massachusetts. But the nation's leaders had not forgotten him. In 1809, President James Madison appointed Adams the minister to Russia. Adams and his family soon left for St. Petersburg.

At home, the War of 1812 broke out against Britain. The British had been kidnapping American sailors at sea, claiming that they were **deserters** from the British navy. Since Russia and Great Britain were **allies,** John Quincy spent most of his time in St. Petersburg explaining to the Russians why the United States was at war with Great Britain. He won the trust and respect of the Russian leaders. In 1814, U.S. officials asked Adams to travel to Ghent, Belgium. There he would **negotiate** a peace **treaty** with Great Britain.

In 1807, John Quincy voted against the Federalist Party by supporting Jefferson's embargo against the British. Abigail Adams was shocked by her son's vote. It "staggered my belief," she wailed. John Quincy countered, "I could wish to please my parents, but my duty I *must* do."

Abigail Adams sent many letters to John Quincy. Her letters contained frequent reminders that he should stay true to his ideals, be good, and dress neatly.

John Quincy Adams (right) shakes hands with a British official after signing the Treaty of Ghent. The treaty ended the War of 1812.

Adams and British officials spent much time "erasing, patching, and mending" the agreement between the two nations. Finally, they signed the Treaty of Ghent on Christmas Eve, 1814. The War of 1812 was over. President Madison then named Adams minister to Great Britain, a position his father had held after the Revolution. When James Monroe was elected the fifth president in 1816, he appointed Adams **secretary of state.** Adams and his family returned to the United States, this time to stay.

Adams's experience as a diplomat helped make him a skillful secretary of state. At this time, the United States controlled much of Florida, but Spain still held the eastern part of it. In 1819, Adams negotiated a treaty with Spain. The Spanish agreed to give up their land in Florida for $5 million. The following year, the **territory** of Missouri wanted to join the **Union.** Southern slave owners wanted Missouri to enter as a slave state. Adams was firmly against slavery. He convinced President Monroe to approve the Missouri Compromise of 1820. This agreement admitted Missouri as a slave state only if Maine entered as a free state, where slavery was illegal.

During Monroe's second term as president, European countries were trying to control parts of South and Central America. The United States did not want Europe to gain power in any part of the Americas.

John Quincy Adams (far left) served as secretary of state under President James Monroe (standing) for eight years.

In 1824, Louisa Adams gave a ball in honor of Andrew Jackson (center). John Quincy was not comfortable at parties, so Louisa always stayed close to him, helping him make polite conversation. She would steer him away when he began to get irritated with an opinion that did not match his own.

Three members of the Adams family served as minister to Great Britain. John Adams became the first U.S. minister to Great Britain following the Revolutionary War. John Quincy Adams served as minister to Great Britain after the War of 1812. And John Quincy's son Charles held the position during the American Civil War.

In 1823, Adams and President Monroe wrote the Monroe **Doctrine,** which warned Europeans not to attempt to colonize any part of North, Central, or South America.

Adams's success as secretary of state impressed many people. Some urged him to run for president in 1824. Andrew Jackson, a war hero who had led American forces at the Battle of New Orleans during the War of 1812, was already a candidate. Adams knew that Jackson was more popular with the American people.

Despite this, he decided to run, though he refused to **campaign** for votes. He wanted people to vote for him because they believed he would be a good president, not because he campaigned for the job. He also believed he deserved the office and that it should be given to him as a reward for his years of service to the country.

When the votes were counted, Andrew Jackson had won the popular vote, which means that more citizens voted for him than for his opponents. But no candidate had won a majority of **electoral votes.** When this happens, the House of Representatives chooses the president. It was a close vote in the House. By only one vote, John Quincy Adams became the sixth president of the United States.

This political cartoon about the 1824 presidential election shows John Quincy Adams (brown coat) and Andrew Jackson (blue coat) sprinting toward the finish line. Between them is former senator William Crawford of Georgia, who was also running for president.

A WOMAN OF THE TIME

John Quincy Adams was a brilliant man with an excellent education. He spoke French, Russian, and German and could read both Greek and Latin. His wife, Louisa, was never given the opportunity to receive such an education. Women of the day were raised to be homemakers and hostesses. Girls from wealthy families were taught how to enter a room with grace, how to sit, and how to talk about acceptable topics. While John Quincy was poring over his books, Louisa was learning proper table manners and a ladylike curtsy. Fortunately, Louisa's parents also saw the value in teaching their daughter music and literature. She learned to play the harp, and she loved to read. She also sang and wrote poetry. Louisa may not have had the same education as her husband, but she was determined to be more than just a pretty face at his parties. From 1818 until 1825, she campaigned to help her husband become president. Although naturally shy, she visited the wives of congressmen, attended parties and balls, and gave many parties of her own. John Quincy was considered cold and sometimes even rude, so Louisa's efforts were important. Her charm and personality won the couple many friends in Washington. Without her help, he might never have become president.

CHAPTER THREE

A BITTER PRESIDENCY

On March 4, 1825, John Quincy Adams spoke at his **inauguration.** He had received only one-third of the popular vote, and he knew that many people wanted Andrew Jackson to be their president. Still, he promised he would work "with a heart devoted to the welfare of the country."

Although John Quincy Adams won the presidency, he failed to win the cooperation of Congress. This kept him from reaching his goals as president.

After moving into the White House, Adams established a daily routine. He would rise at 5 a.m. (4:15 a.m. in the summer) and walk four miles (6 km) before breakfast. In the heat of summer, he often went swimming in the Potomac River near the White House. Once, he had to jump out of a sinking rowboat into the river. Rumors spread that he had drowned.

John Quincy and Louisa's four years in the White House were difficult. He found it hard to achieve his goals. Although Andrew Jackson had not won the election, he had many supporters in Congress. They often voted against Adams. Everyone assumed that Andrew Jackson would win the presidency in the next election. Still, Adams was determined to do his best while he had the chance.

This illustration shows a view of the White House from the Potomac River. As president, John Quincy Adams enjoyed gardening, taking walks near the White House, and swimming in the river.

Before becoming secretary of state, Henry Clay was the Speaker of the House of Representatives. The speaker is the most important person in the House. Clay was famed for his powerful speeches.

Adams wanted the **federal** government to take an active role in helping the states. He proposed the "American System," a plan to make the nation **self-sufficient.** He wanted Americans to buy more American-made goods and fewer foreign goods. Adams's secretary of state, Henry Clay, suggested raising **tariffs** on foreign goods. This would make foreign products more expensive, so Americans would be more likely to buy American-made products. As part of his American System, Adams also proposed building new roads and canals in the South and the West. These would make it easier to transport crops from these regions to the East Coast.

John Adams and John Quincy Adams were the first father and son to both serve as U.S. president. It took 175 years for this to happen again. George W. Bush, the son of George H. W. Bush, became the 43rd U.S. president in 2001. His father was the 41st president.

The Erie Canal (above) was completed in 1825, during John Quincy Adams's presidency. This waterway stretched 363 miles (584 km) across New York State from the Hudson River to Lake Erie. The canal made it much easier to transport goods from the Midwest to the East.

Congressmen blocked Adams's American System. Some did so because they wanted to be sure that Andrew Jackson would win in the next election. Others believed that Adams's plans gave the federal government too much power. In the end, Congress accepted only two of the American System ideas. One was to improve roads in Ohio. The other was to build a canal that connected the Ohio River in the Midwest with the Chesapeake Bay on the East Coast.

Adams also had little support from Congress in **foreign affairs.** His work on the Monroe Doctrine had helped create friendship between the United States and Latin America. In his second year as president,

Latin American leaders planned the Panama Congress. This event was organized to build friendly ties between American nations and establish a united force to fight unfriendly countries. Mexico and Colombia asked the United States to send representatives to this meeting.

President Adams and Secretary of State Henry Clay believed that the United States should take part in the Panama Congress. After all, the United States was the most powerful nation in the Americas. They also wanted to promote friendship and trade between Latin America and the United States. But Congress opposed sending representatives to the meeting. Southern congressmen objected because the Latin American countries had outlawed slavery. Other American leaders said the Panama Congress went against the U.S. policy of remaining **neutral.** In the end, the United States did not take part in the Panama Congress.

When Adams began his presidency, there was only one major political party in the United States: the Democratic-Republicans. Although Adams led this party, many people in the party disagreed with him, and the party split into two groups. Adams's supporters called themselves the National Republicans. The other group, which supported Andrew Jackson, called themselves the Democrats.

It was a difficult time for Adams. To make matters worse, in 1826, Adams learned that his father was very ill. He rushed to Massachusetts to see him. Sadly, he arrived after his father had died. John Quincy Adams said the death struck like "an arrow to my heart."

Work on the nation's first steam-powered locomotive began during John Quincy Adams's presidency.

John Quincy Adams and his father, John Adams, were the only presidents so crushed by the manner and bitterness of their defeat that they refused to attend the inauguration of the winner.

Despite the difficulties, Adams ran for reelection. As the next presidential election drew closer, Jackson's supporters began telling lies about Adams. They called him a snob who hated the American people. They said he lived a life of **luxury** in the White House. To fight back, Adams's supporters claimed that Andrew Jackson was a murderer and a slave trader who was always ready for a fistfight. But few Americans seemed to care that Jackson was an uneducated military man and a slave owner. When the votes were counted, Jackson had won.

John Adams died at age 91. He had spent the final 26 years of his life writing. He once said, "Old minds are like old horses; you must exercise them if you wish to keep them in working order."

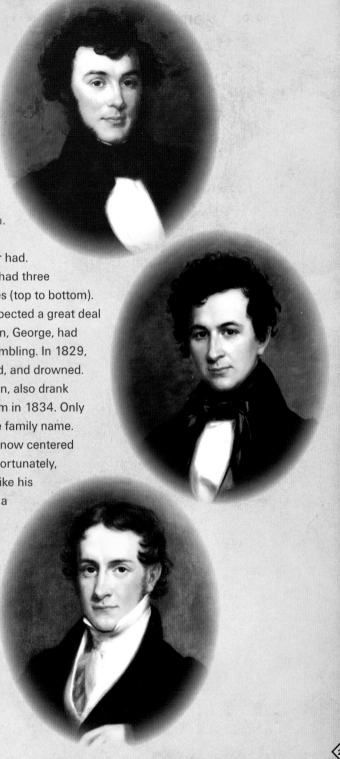

A TROUBLED FAMILY

John Quincy Adams had two younger brothers, Thomas and Charles. All three Adamses struggled with their parents' high expectations. Thomas and Charles led difficult lives. They both struggled with alcoholism. Only John Quincy was able to succeed in politics as his father had.

John Quincy Adams also had three sons, George, John, and Charles (top to bottom). Like his father, John Quincy expected a great deal from his children. His oldest son, George, had problems with drinking and gambling. In 1829, he was on a ship, fell overboard, and drowned. John Quincy's second son, John, also drank heavily. He died from alcoholism in 1834. Only Charles was left to carry on the family name. "All my hopes in this world are now centered upon him," said John Quincy. Fortunately, Charles found success in life. Like his father and grandfather, he had a brilliant career in politics. First, he was a congressman. Then, during the American Civil War, he was appointed minister to Great Britain.

DUTY TO THE END

John Quincy Adams lost the election of 1828. He and Louisa gathered their belongings to leave the White House. Adams thought he had reached the end of his political career. "My own career is closed," he wrote in his diary. "The sun of my political life sets in the deepest gloom."

Moses Billings painted this portrait of John Quincy Adams in 1846. Years after he left office, Adams described his presidency as "the four most miserable years of my life."

Once again, John Quincy returned to the family farm. And once again, the citizens of Massachusetts wanted him to take a seat in Congress. Some people wondered whether the former president should run for the House of Representatives. After all, he had held the most important position in the country. But when they asked Adams if he would consider it, he said, "No person should be **degraded** by serving the people as a Representative in Congress. Nor, in my opinion would a former President of the United States be degraded by serving as a **selectman** of his town." Adams agreed to run. When the votes were counted on November 6, 1830, he had won easily.

After leaving the presidency, John Quincy Adams went home to the family farm in Quincy, Massachusetts. He was born in the house shown here on the left. His father was born next door.

John Quincy Adams is the only former president to be elected to the House of Representatives.

Adams was pleased that people in Massachusetts still believed he was a good leader. "My election as President of the United States was not half as gratifying," he wrote in his diary the night of the election. "No election or appointment conferred upon me ever gave me so much pleasure."

At the age of 64, Adams entered the House of Representatives as a new congressman, representing about 50,000 people from Massachusetts. He earned a salary of $8 a day plus a travel allowance.

His most important goal as a congressman was to fight slavery. He introduced many **petitions** to end it. Southern congressmen wanted to stop him. They created rules (called "gag rules") that kept any item

Adams disliked Andrew Jackson (right). He thought Jackson had bad manners and was poorly educated.

Adams served in the U.S. House of Representatives for 17 years. When Adams was a congressman, the Capitol building had only a small dome rather than the grand dome it has today.

opposing slavery from being read to Congress. But Adams would not give up. He continued sending petitions to the House during the eight years the gag rules were in effect. Congress finally reopened discussions on the issue of slavery in 1844.

Adams also opposed slavery in other ways. In 1841, he worked briefly as a lawyer to defend a group of enslaved Africans. They had taken over a slave ship called the *Amistad*. When the U.S. Navy captured the men, the government had to decide what to do with them. Adams used his skills as a lawyer to defend the men to the Supreme Court, the nation's most powerful court. He won their freedom, and they eventually returned to Africa.

In the House of Representatives, John Quincy Adams became known as a great speaker. His fellow congressmen called him "Old Man **Eloquent**."

THE *AMISTAD* AFFAIR

The Spanish ship *Amistad* (ah-mee-STAHD) was carrying 53 enslaved Africans in the summer of 1839. Slave traders had kidnapped them from Africa, transported them to the island of Cuba, and then sold them to work at sugar plantations. The Africans were on their way to a life of slavery.

Then Cinque (CHIN-kway), one of the Africans, managed to free himself. He and the others took control of the ship. For two months, they sailed up the North American coast. The journey was difficult. They were low on food and water, and they were not experienced at sailing ships. Finally, the U.S. Navy took control of the *Amistad* and captured the African men.

For two years, American abolitionists demanded that the men be freed and returned to Africa. At the same time, Spanish officials and the planters who had bought the enslaved men demanded that their "property" be returned. Finally, the case was sent to the Supreme Court, the most powerful court in the country. The abolitionists asked John Quincy Adams to defend the Africans. At first, he refused. He was older and did not feel up to the challenge. Finally, he agreed, saying, "If, by the blessing of God, my health and strength shall permit, I will argue the case before the Supreme Court."

On the first day of his argument, he turned to the judges and pointed to a copy of the Declaration of Independence that hung across the room. He reminded those present that the

Declaration states, "All men are created equal." He said that these words should apply to the African men he was defending.

The Supreme Court took about one month to make a decision. The judges decided that the Africans had been illegally captured and must be set free. Abolitionists then raised money to help send the men home. The 35 surviving men from the *Amistad* arrived back home in Africa about three years after they were first captured. Cinque is shown in the painting above.

This photograph of John Quincy Adams was taken in 1843.

Adams once sent 350 petitions opposing slavery to the House in a single day. Many of these remained in the basement of the Capitol. In fact, a historian once discovered a janitor using them to light a fire in the Capitol's furnace.

In his later years, Adams also spoke out for the rights of Native Americans. He fought for freedom of speech. He encouraged scientific studies to increase knowledge. As a congressman for 17 straight years, John Quincy Adams became one of the most respected men in Washington, D.C.

Adams once swore he would die while serving his country. This promise came true. On February 21, 1848, Adams gasped and slumped in his seat at the

Capitol. He had suffered a **stroke.** He was carried to a nearby room where he remained for the next two days. His doctors believed he was too ill to be moved, so the lifelong politician died in the U.S. Capitol. He was 80 years old. Louisa Adams lived another four years. She died on May 15, 1852, and was buried at her husband's side.

From his teenage years as his father's secretary to his time as an elderly congressman, Adams served his country. His parents had thrust him into that role. They wanted him to succeed even beyond his father's accomplishments. At his funeral, a senator said what many were thinking: "Where could death have found him, but at the post of duty?"

When Harvard University planned to give President Andrew Jackson an honorary degree, Adams was invited to the ceremony. He replied with a shudder, "I could not be present to see my Darling Harvard disgrace herself by conferring a doctor's degree upon a barbarian and savage who can scarcely spell his own name."

Adams tried to get up after he collapsed in the House chambers, but he fell back into his chair. He died at the Capitol, serving his country to the end.

Time Line

1767
On July 11, John Quincy Adams is born in Braintree, Massachusetts (which later became a part of Quincy). He is the first son of John and Abigail Adams.

1775
The American Revolution begins on April 19. In June, seven-year-old John Quincy climbs Penn Hill to watch the Battle of Bunker Hill from a distance.

1778
The Continental Congress sends John Adams on a mission to France. John Quincy goes with him and acts as his secretary.

1781
John Quincy, who now speaks perfect French, works as a secretary and translator for an American diplomat in Russia. (French was the language used by diplomats at the time.)

1782
John Quincy tours Europe.

1783
In April, John Quincy travels to the Netherlands to serve as his father's secretary.

1785
John Quincy returns to the United States and enrolls at Harvard.

1790
John Quincy Adams opens his first law office.

1794
President George Washington appoints John Quincy Adams minister to the Netherlands.

1796
John Adams is elected president.

1797
John Quincy Adams marries Louisa Catherine Johnson on July 26. President John Adams appoints John Quincy Adams minister to Prussia, now part of Germany.

1801
John Adams leaves the presidency. John Quincy Adams and his family return to the United States.

1802
John Quincy Adams is elected a U.S. senator from Massachusetts. He is a member of the Federalist Party.

1808
During his time as senator, John Quincy Adams angers the Federalists by siding too often with President Thomas Jefferson, a Democratic-Republican. The Federalists meet in Boston and select a candidate to replace Adams in the next Senate election.

1809
President James Madison appoints John Quincy Adams minister to Russia.

1812
The United States begins fighting the War of 1812 against Great Britain.

1814
John Quincy Adams leads the American team that forges a peace treaty with Great Britain.

1816
James Monroe is elected the fifth president. He appoints John Quincy Adams his secretary of state.

1819
John Quincy Adams negotiates the purchase of eastern Florida from Spain for $5 million.

1820
President Monroe signs the Missouri Compromise in 1820 at the urging of John Quincy Adams.

1823
The Monroe Doctrine is drafted by President Monroe with the help of John Quincy Adams.

1824
John Quincy Adams runs for president. None of the four candidates wins a majority, so the House of Representatives must choose the president.

1825
The U.S. House of Representatives selects John Quincy Adams to be the sixth president. Andrew Jackson, who had won the popular vote, begins campaigning immediately for the next election. Adams's inauguration takes place on March 4. During the next four years, Adams will attempt to adopt the "American System," which is intended to make the nation more self-sufficient. Many congressmen oppose Adams's plans.

1826
Adams wants to send American representatives to the Panama Congress, an event organized to build friendly ties among American nations, but the U.S. Congress refuses. Adams's father, former president John Adams, dies on July 4, the 50th anniversary of the signing of the Declaration of Independence.

1828
Andrew Jackson is elected the seventh president of the United States. John Quincy Adams retires, thinking his career in politics is finished.

1830
Friends convince Adams to run for Congress. At age 63, he is elected to the House of Representatives. He will spend the next 17 years as a congressman.

1836
Adams sends many petitions against slavery to the House of Representatives. Southern congressmen create "gag rules" to stop all petitions against slavery from being heard in Congress.

1841
Adams pleads the case for a group of enslaved Africans who took over a Spanish slave ship, the *Amistad*. He wins, and the Africans are set free. Abolitionists eventually help them return to Africa.

1844
Thanks to Adams's efforts, the "gag rules" are overturned. Congress may again consider antislavery petitions.

1848
On February 21, John Quincy Adams is at the Capitol when he collapses from a stroke. He dies two days later.

GLOSSARY

abolitionists (ab-uh-LISH-uh-nists)
Abolitionists were people who wanted to end slavery in the United States. Abolitionists fought to help the Africans who took over the Spanish slave ship *Amistad*.

alcoholism (AL-kuh-hall-ih-zum) Alcoholism is when a person drinks too much alcohol and is unable to control the amount he or she drinks. Both of John Quincy Adams's brothers struggled with alcoholism.

allies (AL-lyze) Allies are nations that have agreed to help each other by fighting together against a common enemy. Great Britain and Russia were allies during the War of 1812.

campaign (kam-PAYN) A campaign is the process of running for an election, including activities such as giving speeches or attending rallies. John Quincy Adams refused to campaign for the presidency.

candidate (KAN-duh-dayt) A candidate is a person running in an election. The Federalists selected a new candidate for senator when John Quincy Adams sided with the Democratic-Republicans.

Continental Congress (kon-tih-NEN-tul KONG-gris) The Continental Congress was the group of men who governed the United States during and after the Revolution. John Adams was a member of the First Continental Congress.

degraded (dee-GRAY-ded) If a person is degraded, he or she is dishonored or shamed. John Quincy Adams said a former president was not degraded by accepting a smaller position in the government.

deserters (di-ZER-turz) Deserters are people who leave the military without permission. The British searched American ships for sailors they thought had deserted their navy.

diplomat (DIP-luh-mat) A diplomat is a government official whose job is to represent a country in discussions with other countries. Both John Quincy Adams and his father were diplomats.

doctrine (DOK-trin) A doctrine is something that a nation, religion, or other group firmly believes. John Quincy Adams helped President Monroe create the Monroe Doctrine.

electoral votes (ee-LEKT-uh-rul VOHTS) Electoral votes are those cast by representatives of the American public for the president and vice president. Each state chooses representatives who vote for a candidate in an election. These representatives vote according to what the majority of people in their state want.

eloquent (EL-oh-kwent) If people are eloquent, they express themselves well. John Quincy Adams was known as "Old Man Eloquent" when he was in the House of Representatives.

embargo (em-BAR-goh) An embargo stops one country from selling its goods to another country. The United States began an embargo against Britain in 1807.

expectations (ek-spek-TAY-shunz) If people have high expectations, they expect good things from someone or something. Abigail and John Adams had high expectations for their son.

federal (FE-dur-ul) Federal means having to do with the central government of the United States, rather than a state or city government. John Quincy Adams wanted the federal government to help the states.

foreign affairs (FOR-un uh-FAYRZ) Foreign affairs are matters involving other (foreign) countries. Congress refused to support John Quincy Adams in foreign affairs.

inauguration (ih-naw-gyuh-RAY-shun)
An inauguration is the ceremony that takes place when a new president begins a term. John Quincy Adams's inauguration took place on March 4, 1825.

luxury (LUK-shur-ee) Luxury is great comfort and pleasure. Andrew Jackson's supporters accused Adams of living a life of luxury at the White House.

minister (MIN-uh-stur) A minister is a person who represents one country in another country. Both John Quincy Adams and his father served as minister to Great Britain.

negotiate (ni-GOH-she-ayt) If people negotiate, they talk things over and try to come to an agreement. John Quincy Adams went to Ghent to negotiate a treaty with Great Britain.

neutral (NOO-trul) If people are neutral, they do not take sides. Some people thought the Panama Congress went against the U.S. policy of remaining neutral.

petitions (puh-TISH-unz) Petitions are written requests or demands for something. Congressmen send petitions to be heard by other members of Congress.

political parties (puh-LIT-uh-kul PAR-teez) Political parties are groups of people who share similar ideas about how to run a government. The two major political parties in the early years of the nation were the Federalists and the Democratic-Republicans.

politics (PAWL-uh-tiks) Politics refers to the actions and practices of the government. John Quincy Adams and his father were both active in politics.

resigned (ree-ZYND) If people resigned, they gave up their jobs. John Quincy Adams resigned from the Senate when the Federalists supported another candidate.

revolution (rev-uh-LOO-shun) A revolution is something that causes a complete change in government. The American Revolution was a war fought between the United States and Great Britain.

secretary of state (SEK-ruh-tayr-ee OF STAYT) The secretary of state is a close adviser to the president. He or she is involved with the nation's relationships with other countries.

selectman (si-LEKT-man) A selectman is a person elected to a town's government. John Quincy Adams said it was not a disgrace for a former president to serve as a selectman.

self-sufficient (SELF-suh-FISH-unt) If people are self-sufficient, they do not need help from others. John Quincy Adams wanted the United States to be self-sufficient.

stroke (STROHK) A stroke is a sudden injury to the brain when a blood vessel breaks or becomes blocked. John Quincy Adams died from a stroke.

tariffs (TAYR-ifs) Tariffs are taxes on goods that are brought in from another country. Secretary of State Henry Clay suggested raising tariffs on foreign goods.

territory (TAYR-uh-tor-ee) A territory is a land or region, especially land that belongs to a government. The territory of Missouri joined the Union as a slave state.

translator (TRANS-lay-tur) A translator changes words from one language to another. John Quincy Adams translated French into English for an American diplomat.

treaty (TREE-tee) A treaty is a formal agreement between nations. The United States signed a peace treaty with Great Britain after the American Revolution.

Union (YOON-yen) A union is the joining together of people or groups of people, such as states. The Union is another name for the United States.

THE UNITED STATES GOVERNMENT

The United States government is divided into three equal branches: the executive, the legislative, and the judicial. This division helps prevent abuses of power because each branch has to answer to the other two. No one branch can become too powerful.

EXECUTIVE BRANCH

PRESIDENT
VICE PRESIDENT
DEPARTMENTS

The job of the executive branch is to enforce the laws. It is headed by the president, who serves as the spokesperson for the United States around the world. The president signs bills into law and appoints important officials such as federal judges. He or she is also the commander in chief of the U.S. military. The president is assisted by the vice president, who takes over if the president dies or cannot carry out the duties of the office.

The executive branch also includes various departments, each focused on a specific topic. They include the Defense Department, the Justice Department, and the Agriculture Department. The department heads, along with other officials such as the vice president, serve as the president's closest advisers, called the cabinet.

LEGISLATIVE BRANCH

CONGRESS
Senate and
House of Representatives

The job of the legislative branch is to make the laws. It consists of Congress, which is divided into two parts: the Senate and the House of Representatives. The Senate has 100 members, and the House of Representatives has 435 members. Each state has two senators. The number of representatives a state has varies depending on the state's population.

Besides making laws, Congress also passes budgets and enacts taxes. In addition, it is responsible for declaring war, maintaining the military, and regulating trade with other countries.

JUDICIAL BRANCH

SUPREME COURT
COURTS OF APPEALS
DISTRICT COURTS

The job of the judicial branch is to interpret the laws. It consists of the nation's federal courts. Trials are held in district courts. During trials, judges must decide what laws mean and how they apply. Courts of appeals review the decisions made in district courts.

The nation's highest court is the Supreme Court. If someone disagrees with a court of appeals ruling, he or she can ask the Supreme Court to review it. The Supreme Court may refuse. The Supreme Court makes sure that decisions and laws do not violate the Constitution.

CHOOSING
THE PRESIDENT

It may seem odd, but American voters don't elect the president directly. Instead, the president is chosen using what is called the Electoral College.

Each state gets as many votes in the Electoral College as its combined total of senators and representatives in Congress. For example, Iowa has two senators and five representatives, so it gets seven electoral votes. Although the District of Columbia does not have any voting members in Congress, it gets three electoral votes. Usually, the candidate who wins the most votes in any given state receives all of that state's electoral votes.

To become president, a candidate must get more than half of the Electoral College votes. There are a total of 538 votes in the Electoral College, so a candidate needs 270 votes to win. If nobody receives 270 Electoral College votes, the House of Representatives chooses the president.

With the Electoral College system, the person who receives the most votes nationwide does not always receive the most electoral votes. This happened most recently in 2000, when Al Gore received half a million more national votes than George W. Bush. Bush became president because he had more Electoral College votes.

THE WHITE HOUSE

The White House is the official home of the president of the United States. It is located at 1600 Pennsylvania Avenue NW in Washington, D.C. In 1792, a contest was held to select the architect who would design the president's home. James Hoban won. Construction took eight years.

The first president, George Washington, never lived in the White House. The second president, John Adams, moved into the house in 1800, though the inside was not yet complete. During the War of 1812, British soldiers burned down much of the White House. It was rebuilt several years later.

The White House was changed through the years. Porches were added, and President Theodore Roosevelt added the West Wing. President William Taft changed the shape of the presidential office, making it into the famous Oval Office. While Harry Truman was president, the old house was discovered to be structurally weak. All the walls were reinforced with steel, and the rooms were rebuilt.

Today, the White House has 132 rooms (including 35 bathrooms), 28 fireplaces, and 3 elevators. It takes 570 gallons of paint to cover the outside of the six-story building. The White House provides the president with many ways to relax. It includes a putting green, a jogging track, a swimming pool, a tennis court, and beautifully landscaped gardens. The White House also has a movie theater, a billiard room, and a one-lane bowling alley.

PRESIDENTIAL PERKS

The job of president of the United States is challenging. It is probably one of the most stressful jobs in the world. Because of this, presidents are paid well, though not nearly as well as the leaders of large corporations. In 2007, the president earned $400,000 a year. Presidents also receive extra benefits that make the demanding job a little more appealing.

★ **Camp David:** In the 1940s, President Franklin D. Roosevelt chose this heavily wooded spot in the mountains of Maryland to be the presidential retreat, where presidents can relax. Even though it is a retreat, world business is conducted there. Most famously, President Jimmy Carter met with Middle Eastern leaders at Camp David in 1978. The result was a peace agreement between Israel and Egypt.

★ *Air Force One:* The president flies on a jet called *Air Force One*. It is a Boeing 747-200B that has been modified to meet the president's needs.

Air Force One is the size of a large home. It is equipped with a dining room, sleeping quarters, a conference room, and office space. It also has two kitchens that can provide food for up to 50 people.

★ **The Secret Service:** While not the most glamorous of the president's perks, the Secret Service is one of the most important. The Secret Service is a group of highly trained agents who protect the president and the president's family.

★ **The Presidential State Car:** The presidential limousine is a stretch Cadillac DTS.

It has been armored to protect the president in case of attack. Inside the plush car are a foldaway desk, an entertainment center, and a communications console.

★ **The Food:** The White House has five chefs who will make any food the president wants. The White House also has an extensive wine collection.

★ **Retirement:** A former president receives a pension, or retirement pay, of just under $180,000 a year. Former presidents also receive Secret Service protection for the rest of their lives.

FACTS

QUALIFICATIONS

To run for president, a candidate must

★ be at least 35 years old
★ be a citizen who was born in the United States
★ have lived in the United States for 14 years

TERM OF OFFICE

A president's term of office is four years.
No president can stay in office for more than two terms.

ELECTION DATE

The presidential election takes place every four years on the first Tuesday of November.

INAUGURATION DATE

Presidents are inaugurated on January 20.

OATH OF OFFICE

I do solemnly swear I will faithfully execute the office of the President of the United States and will to the best of my ability preserve, protect, and defend the Constitution of the United States.

WRITE A LETTER TO THE PRESIDENT

One of the best things about being a U.S. citizen is that Americans get to participate in their government. They can speak out if they feel government leaders aren't doing their jobs. They can also praise leaders who are going the extra mile. Do you have something you'd like the president to do? Should the president worry more about the environment and encourage people to recycle? Should the government spend more money on our schools? You can write a letter to the president to say how you feel!

1600 Pennsylvania Avenue
Washington, D.C. 20500
You can even send an e-mail to: president@whitehouse.gov

BOOKS

Burgan, Michael. *John Quincy Adams.* Minneapolis: Compass Point Books, 2003.

Collier, Christopher, and James Lincoln Collier. *Andrew Jackson's America.* New York: Marshall Cavendish, 1999.

Gormley, Beatrice. *First Ladies: Women Who Called the White House Home.* New York: Scholastic, 1997.

McCollum, Sean. *John Quincy Adams: America's 6th President.* New York: Children's Press, 2003.

Somervill, Barbara A. *The Amistad Mutiny: Fighting for Freedom.* Mankato, MN: The Child's World, 2005.

Walker, Jane C. *John Quincy Adams.* Springfield, NJ: Enslow Publishers, 2000.

VIDEOS

The History Channel Presents The Presidents. DVD (New York: A&E Home Video, 2005).

National Geographic's Inside the White House. DVD (Washington, DC: National Geographic Video, 2003).

INTERNET SITES

Visit our Web page for lots of links about John Quincy Adams and other U.S. presidents:

http://www.childsworld.com/links

Note to Parents, Teachers, and Librarians: We routinely verify our Web links to make sure they are safe, active sites—so encourage your readers to check them out!

INDEX